Contents

Introduction

Round-up Starter Grammer Practice combines games and fun with serious, systematic grammer practice. It is ideal for young learners in the preliminary stages of English language learning.

Students see grammer points clearly presented in colourful boxes and tables. They practice grammer through lively, highly illustrated games and activities.

Round-up is especially designed for different students studying English in different ways.

It can be used:
- in class with a coursebook. Students do both oral work - in pairs and in groups - and written work in Round-up.
- after class. The 'write-in' activities are ideal for homework. Students can practice what they have learned in the classroom.
- in the holidays for revision. Round-up has clear instructions and simple grammer boxes, so students can study at home without a teacher.

The Round-up Teacher's Guide includes a full answer key and four tests plus answer keys.

Pearson Education Ltd
Edinburgh Gate, Harlow,
Essex CM20 2JE England
and Associated Companies throughout the world.

www.longman.com

First published in 1994 by E. Vlachou - "Express Publications".
This edition published by Pearson Education Limited 2003.
Eighth impression 2008

Printed in China   SWTC/08

Illustrated by Philip Vazakas and Terry Wilson

ISBN 978-0-582-82349-5

1. The Alphabet

apple

A .A.....................

a...a......................

ball

B .B.....................

b...b......................

cat

C..C....................

c..c......................

doll

D..D....................

d..d......................

egg

E..E....................

e..e......................

fat

F..F....................

f...f......................

| A for apple | C for cat | E for egg |
| B for ball | D for doll | F for fat |

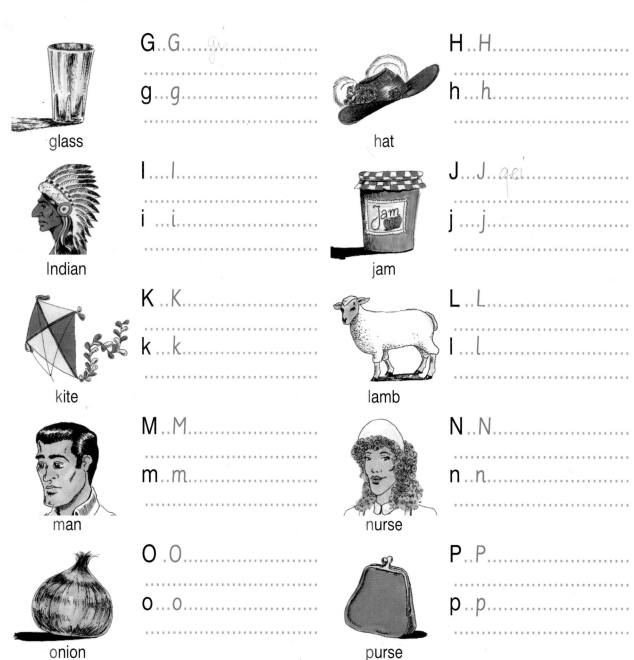

glass

G..G....gr..............................

g...g...................................

H..H....................................

h...h...................................

hat

Indian

I....I..................................

i ...i..................................

J..J...qei..............................

j...j..................................

jam

kite

K..K....................................

k...k...................................

L..L....................................

l...l...................................

lamb

man

M..M....................................

m..m....................................

N..N....................................

n..n....................................

nurse

onion

O..O....................................

o...o...................................

P..P....................................

p..p....................................

purse

G for glass
H for hat
I for Indian
J for jam
K for kite

L for lamb
M for man
N for nurse
O for onion
P for purse

Q ..Q.............................

q ...q.............................

queen

R ..R.............................

r ....r.............................

rain

S ..S.............................

s ....s.............................

star

T .T.............................

t ..t.............................

train

U ..U.............................

u ...u.............................

umbrella

V ...V.............................

v ...v.............................

van

W .W.............................

w ..w.............................

watch

X ..X.............................

x ...x.............................

box

Y ..Y.............................

y ..y.............................

yacht

Z .Z.............................

z ..z.............................

zoo

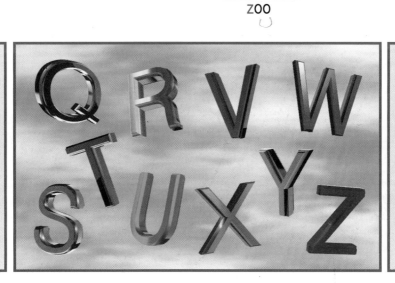

Q for queen	W for watch
R for rain	X for box
S for star	Y for yacht
T for train	Z for zoo
U for umbrella	I can learn it
V for van	You can too!

1. The Alphabet

 Fill in the missing letters.

A, a *A, a*		_ _ ple	N, n *N, n*		_ ur _ e
B, b *B, b*		_ _ ll	O, o *O, o*		_ ni _ n
C, c *C, c*		_ a _	P, p *P, p*		_ _ rse
D, d *D, d*		_ _ ll	Q, q *Q, q*		_ _ een
E, e *E, e*		_ g _	R, r *R, r*		_ _ in
F, f *F, f*		_ _ t	S, s *S, s*		_ t _ r
G, g *G, g*		_ l _ ss	T, t *T, t*		_ _ ain
H, h *H, h*		_ a _	U, u *U, u*		_ _ brella
I, i *I, i*		_ n _ ian	V, v *V, v*		_ a _
J, j *J, j*		_ a _	W, w *W, w*		_ _ tch
K, k *K, k*		_ _ te	X, x *X, x*		_ o _
L, l *L, l*		_ a _ b	Y, y *Y, y*		_ ach _
M, m *M, m*		_ a _	Z, z *Z, z*		_ o _

2 Fill in the missing small letters.

..*a*.. b ..... d ..... f ..... h ..... j ..... l .....
n ..... p ..... r ..... t ..... v ..... x ..... z

3 Fill in the missing capital letters.

A ..*B*.. C ..... E ..... G I
..... K ..... M ..... O ..... Q .....
S ..... U ..... W ..... Y .....

4 Circle the odd letter.

1. a a a (u) a a
2. p p q p p p
3. d d d b d d

4. s s s c s s
5. v u v v v v
6. n n n m n n

7. b b b b d b
8. s z s s s s
9. u u v u u u

5 Write in capital letters.

1. dog ..*DOG*.........
2. apple ....
3. umbrella ....
4. jam ....
5. queen ....

6. watch ....
7. lamb ....
8. train ....
9. cat ....
10. glass ....

6 Write in small letters.

1. CAT ...*cat*...........
2. EGG ....
3. NURSE ....
4. YACHT ....
5. KITE ....

6. ONION ....
7. ZOO ....
8. PURSE ....
9. TRAIN ....
10. FAT ....

(7) **Correct the words.**

1. boll ... *doll* ....
2. opple ....
3. vmbrella......................

4. nat ....
5. nan........................
6. iam ....

7. pueen........................
8. uatch ....
9. jamb........................

(8) **Repeat after your teacher.**

th / ð / or / θ /	this, that, them, there, they, thin, thief, three, thing
ch / tʃ /	chart, cherry, chess, child, church, chin, chair
ph / f /	phone, photo, Philip
sh / ʃ /	ship, shop, shell, shut, shoe, shot

Alphabet Games

1. The teacher shows alphabet flashcards to the pupils. Pupils in teams identify the letters, then say a word starting with this letter. Each correct answer scores 1 point.

   Team A P1: (shows card with letter "m")   Team B P1: (shows card with letter "b")
   Team B P1: "m" for man   Team A P2: "b" for ball   etc

2. The teacher shows word flashcards to the pupils. Teams in turn spell the word shown. Each correct spelling scores 1 point. The team with the most points is the winner.

   Teacher: (shows "cat")   Teacher: (shows "train")
   Team A P1: c–a–t   Team B P1: t–r–a–i–n   etc

2. A - An

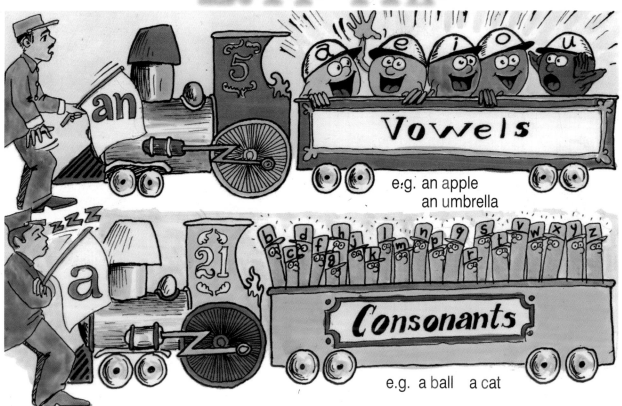

e.g. an apple
an umbrella

e.g. a ball   a cat

9 Circle the vowels.

c, d, (a), g, k, i, l, m, o, p, q, w, e, x, s, z, u, f

10 Repeat after your teacher.

a + ll / ɔː /	ball, call, small, all, tall, fall
c + a, o, u / k /	cat, cost, cup, coffee, coat, can
c + e, i, y / s /	cell, cinema, cycle, city, certain
e is silent at the end	make, bake, snake, cake, apple, Coke, kite
ee / iː /	bee, sheep, see, feet, seed, meet

11 Fill in: a or an.

1. ......*a*...... dog   2. .... book   3. .... elephant   4. .... octopus

2. A – An

5. .... house   6. .... fish   7. .... aeroplane   8. .... banana

9. .... boy   10. .... rabbit   11. .... ear   12. .... orange

13. .... insect   14. .... pen   15. .... ice-cream   16. .... desk

  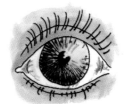 

17. .... table   18. .... snake   19. .... eye   20. .... pencil

(12) Repeat after your teacher.

k is not pronounced before n	knit, knife, know, knee
oo / ʊ / or / u: /	book, cook, good, pool, moon **but:** door, floor
q + u / kw /	queen, quit, question
y / j / at the beginning	yes, yellow, yacht
y / ɪ / at the end or / aɪ / in one syllable words	Mary, tidy, Sally, cherry, sky, fly, dry, spy, cry
s / z / between vowels	rose, close, rise

13 Fill in: a or an.

..*an*... owl

..... eagle

..... monkey

..... tiger

..... giraffe

..... elephant

..... girl

..... ostrich

..... zebra

..... lion

..... kangaroo

..... mouse

..... crocodile

..... frog

..... flower

..... bee

Game 3

The pupils look at the picture for Ex. 13 for 3 minutes. Then the pupils close their books and teams in turn try to remember as many things as possible using "a" or "an". Each correct item gets 1 point. The team with the most points is the winner.

Team A P1: a flower	Team A P2: a ostrich
Team B P1: a tiger	Teacher: No! **an** ostrich. Team B doesn't get a point.

Game 4

Pupils look at Ex. 11 and play the game "I spy with my little eye ...".

Teacher: I spy with my little eye something beginning with "b".
Team A P1: boy (banana/book etc)   etc

3. Numbers

One, two, three
you and me

four, five, six, seven
angels in heaven

eight, nine, ten
say it again.

1 one	7 seven	13 thirteen	19 nineteen	70 seventy
2 two	8 eight	14 fourteen	20 twenty	80 eighty
3 three	9 nine	15 fifteen	30 thirty	90 ninety
4 four	10 ten	16 sixteen	40 forty	100 a hundred
5 five	11 eleven	17 seventeen	50 fifty	
6 six	12 twelve	18 eighteen	60 sixty	

(14) Fill in the missing numbers.

one ..*two*... .... five .... eight .... ten
.... twelve .... seventeen ....

(15) Count the stars and write the numbers.

1. ✷✷✷✷ .....*four*............. 5. ✷✷✷✷✷✷ ....
2. ✷✷✷✷✷✷✷✷✷ .... 6. ✷✷✷✷✷✷✷✷✷✷ ....
3. ✷✷✷ .... 7. ✷✷✷✷✷✷✷✷✷✷✷ ....
4. ✷✷✷✷✷ .... 8. ✷✷✷✷✷✷✷✷✷✷✷✷✷✷ ....

Game 5

Pupils start a counting chain from 1-20 round the class. Any pupil who cannot say a number is out of the game. The pupils who remain at the end are the winners.

4. Plural Form

Singular	Plural

one flower	three flowers

s, ss, sh, ch, x, o ➡ **es**	box boxes

one bus   two bus**es**

consonant + y ➡ **ies** **vowel (a, e, i, o, u) + y** ➡ **s**	lady ladies boy boys

one baby   two babies

(16) Fill in the plural as in the example:

1. One hat. Two ...*hats*.......   2. One witch. Two ....   3. One fly. Two ....

4. One tomato. Two ....   5. One brush. Two ....   6. One bird. Two ....

4. Plural Form

7. One glass. Two .... 8. One spy. Two .... 9. One rabbit. Two ....

10. One fox. Two .... 11. One ostrich. Two .... 12. One toy. Two ....

Irregular Plurals

One man. Two men.   One woman. Two women.   One child. Two children.

One foot. Two feet.   One tooth. Two teeth.   One goose. Two geese.

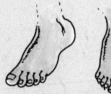 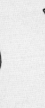

One mouse. Two mice.   One fish. Two fish.   One sheep. Two sheep.

17 **Write the plural form.**

1. cat ....._cats_......... 6. fish .... 11. goose ....
2. child .... 7. woman .... 12. spy ....
3. foot .... 8. lion .... 13. watch ....
4. tooth .... 9. mouse .... 14. star ....
5. eye .... 10. pencil .... 15. van ....

(18) Fill in the plural as in the example:

1. One potato. Two *potatoes*   2. One strawberry. Two ....   3. One basket. Two ....

4. One peach. Two ....   5. One dish. Two ....   6. One tree. Two ....

(19) Find the differences in picture B.

.... 2 women, 3 children etc. ....

 Game 6

Pupils in teams look at picture B for Ex. 19 for 3 minutes.
Then they close their books and try to remember as many things as possible.

5. Personal Pronouns

Singular	Plural
I	we
you	you
he, she, it	they

People	Animals	Things
He / She	It	It
man 	bird 	ball
boy	horse	book
woman	mouse	rubber 
girl	tiger	chair

We say **he** for men and boys, **she** for women and girls and **it** for things. We also say **it** for animals when we do not know their sex.

20 Fill in: I, he, she, it, we or they.

21 Fill in: he, she, it, we or they.

1. Maria	*...she....*	6. you and I	....	11. woman	....
2. Peter	....	7. apples	....	12. purse	....
3. hat	....	8. octopus	....	13. Tom and I	....
4. girl	....	9. boy	....	14. snake	....
5. buses	....	10. Kim and John	....	15. witch	....

 Game 7

The teacher divides the class into two teams and shows them people or things. The teams in turn say the correct personal pronoun. Each correct answer gets 1 point. The team with the most points is the winner. You can also play the game by showing the pupils pictures from magazines.

Teacher:	(points to Ann)		Teacher:	(points to some books)
Team A P1:	she		Team B P1:	they etc

6. The Verb "to be"

Affirmative		Negative		Interrogative
Long form	**Short form**	**Long form**	**Short form**	
I am	I'm	I am not	I'm not	Am I?
You are	You're	You are not	You aren't	Are you?
He is	He's	He is not	He isn't	Is he?
She is	She's	She is not	She isn't	Is she?
It is	It's	It is not	It isn't	Is it?
We are	We're	We are not	We aren't	Are we?
You are	You're	You are not	You aren't	Are you?
They are	They're	They are not	They aren't	Are they?

22 **Write as in the example:**

Long form

1. It .. *is* .... a doll.
2. They .... dancers.
3. He .... a teacher.
4. We .... girls.
5. I .... Tony.
6. She .... a singer.

Short form

It 's .... a doll.
They .... dancers.
He .... a teacher.
We .... girls.
I .... Tony.
She .... a singer.

23 Fill in: am, is or are.

1. I ....*am*.... a dancer and you ......*are*..... a singer.

2. We .... football players and they .... acrobats.

3. He .... a mechanic and she .... an engineer.

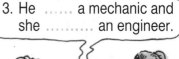

4. I .... a fireman and he .... a policeman.

5. You .... a policewoman and I .... a pilot.

6. We .... pupils and you .... students.

7. I .... a bus driver and you .... a postman.

8. I .... a pilot and he .... a sailor.

9. I .... a doctor and he .... a teacher.

Game 8

Pupils in two teams look at the pictures for Ex. 23 for 2 minutes. Then the teams in turn, with books closed, try to remember as many jobs as possible. The winning team is the one which remembers the most jobs.

Team A P1:	bus driver	Team A P2:	pilot	Team A P3:	doctor	
Team B P1:	postman	Team B P2:	policewoman	Team B P3:	sailor	etc

24 Match column A with column B, then write the sentences.

A	B	
1. I am	A. a box	.....*I am a pupil.*.........................
2. He is	B. Mary	....
3. It is	C. Jim	....
4. She is	D. a pupil	....
5. We are	E. singers	....

6. The Verb "to be"

(25) Ask and answer as in the example:

1. ....*Is he* ... a singer?
   ..No, he isn't a singer....
   .. He is a policeman.......

2. .... pilots?
   ....
   ....

3. .... a postman?
   ....
   ....

4. .... singers?
   ....
   ....

5. .... firemen?
   ....
   ....

6. .... a teacher?
   ....
   ....

Short answers	Am I/are you a pupil?	Yes, I am.	No, I'm not.
	Is he/she/it fat?	Yes, he/she/it is.	No, he/she/it isn't.
	Are we/you they pupils?	Yes, we/you they are.	No, we/you they aren't.

(26) Answer the questions.

1. Are they mechanics?
   ...No, they aren't..........
   ...They're firemen.........

2. Is he a postman?
   ....
   ....

3. Is she a dancer?
   ....
   ....

4. Are you bus drivers?
   ....
   ....

5. Are they acrobats?
   ....
   ....

6. Is it a flower?
   ....
   ....

(27) Write the plural.

 He is a doctor.

 1. *.. They are doctors. ..*

 It is a flower.

 2. ....

 I am a teacher.

 3. ....

 She is a pupil.

 4. ....

 Game 9

The teacher chooses a leader from the class and divides the class into two teams. The leader thinks of a job (eg dancer). The teams in turn ask the leader questions to find his/her job.

Team A P1:	Are you a teacher?		Leader:	No, I'm not.
Leader:	No, I'm not.		Team B P2:	Are you a dancer?
Team B P1:	Are you a doctor?		Leader:	Yes, I am!
Leader:	No, I'm not.		Team B is the winner.	
Team A P2:	Are you a policeman?			

Writing Activity 1

First read about Ann then write about you.

Ann
20
singer
London

Put your photo here

....
....
....
....

I am Ann.
I am twenty.
I am a singer.

....
....
....

Revision Exercises I

28 Fill in: a or an.

1. ..*an*..... elephant 2. .... bee 3. .... snake 4. .... fish

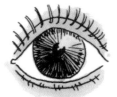   

5. .... eye 6. .... onion 7. .... purse 8. .... owl

29 Fill in: a or an.

.... cloud
.... aeroplane
..*a*.. bird
.... girl
.... apple
.... ball
.... sailor
.... shark
.... boat
.... octopus

30 Count the stars and write the numbers as in the example:

1. ✱✱✱✱✱✱✱✱   ..*eight*............   6. ✱✱✱✱✱   ....
2. ✱✱✱✱✱✱✱✱✱✱   ....   7. ✱✱✱✱✱✱✱✱✱✱✱   ....
3. ✱✱   ....   8. ✱✱✱✱✱✱   ....
4. ✱✱✱✱✱✱   ....   9. ✱✱✱✱✱✱✱✱✱   ....
5. ✱✱✱✱   ....   10. ✱✱✱✱✱✱✱✱✱✱✱✱   ....

(31) Fill in the plural form.

1. One glass. Two *..glasses..*
2. One boy. Two ....
3. One bee. Three ....

4. One foot. Two ....
5. One mouse. Three ....
6. One fish. Four ....

7. One fox. Three ....
8. One umbrella. Two ....
9. One girl. Two ....

(32) Fill in: he, she, it or they.

1. girl ...*she*...............
2. man ....
3. crocodiles ....
4. John ....
5. Helen ....

6. pencils ....
7. women ....
8. boy ....
9. Michael ....
10. tooth ....

(33) Answer the questions.

1. Is she a singer?
   ..No, she isn't................
   ..She's a dancer.............

2. Is he a postman?
   ....
   ....

3. Is she an acrobat?
   ....
   ....

4. Is it a crocodile?
   ....
   ....

5. Is it a kitten?
   ....
   ....

6. Is he a football player?
   ....
   ....

7. Is she a dancer?

8. Is he a policeman?

9. Is he a pilot?

....

....

....

....

....

....

(34) **First read about Jenny then write about your friend.**

Jenny	...I am Jenny........................
27	...I am twenty-seven................
dancer	...I am a dancer...................
Paris	...I am from Paris.................

Put
your friend's
photo here

....

....

....

....

(35) **Fill in: is or are.**

 Julie   Pablo    Simon    Ornella

Julie 1) ..*is*.. twenty-two. She 2) .... a singer. Pablo and Simon 3) .... fifteen. They
4) .... students. Pablo 5) .... from Spain. Julie and Simon 6) .... from England.
Ornella 7) .... twenty-five. She 8) .... from Italy. She 9) .... a policewoman.

(36) **Find the mistakes and correct them.**

1. She is a doctors.   ....*She is a doctor*...........
2. I am an boy.   ....
3. They is flowers.   ....
4. They are bus driver.   ....
5. We is policemen.   ....
6. He is a postwoman.   ....
7. Julie am twelve.   ....
8. They are potatos.   ....
9. They are babys.   ....
10. John and Mary is teachers. ....

7. This – These – That – Those

This is a big egg.

These are crocodile's eggs.

Look! That is a crocodile!

Those are crocodiles. Help!!

This - These (near) ☞	This is a pen.	These are pens.
That - Those (far) ☞	That is a book.	Those are books.

37 Write sentences using This or These.

1. hats
2. skirt
3. shirts
4. dress
5. trousers
6. boots

1. ...*These are hats.* ....

2. ....

3. ....

4. ....

5. ....

6. ....

38 Write sentences using That or Those.

1. ...*That is a bus.* ....
2. ....
3. ....
4. ....
5. ....
6. ....

39 Write what ET asks his friend as in the example:

1. What *is that* ?

It's a snake.

2. What are .... ?

They're monkeys.

3. What .... ?

It's a bee.

4. What .... ?

They're shoes.

5. What .... ?

It's a cake.

6. What .... ?

It's a hat!!!

40 Fill in: this, these, that or those.

1. ...*This*..... is a blue monster.

2. .... is a red monster.

3. .... are yellow monsters.

4. .... are green monsters.

5. .... is a black monster.

6. .... is a white monster.

7. .... are brown monsters.

8. .... is a pink monster.

Game 10

Pupils look at the "coloured monsters" above for three minutes then close their books and try to remember as many monsters as possible. Play the game as in the example:

Team A P1:	This is a white monster.
Team B P1:	This is a white monster and that is a black monster.
Team A P2:	This is a black monster and that is a blue monster.
Team B P2:	This is a blue monster and that is a pink monster. etc

8. "Have (got)"

Affirmative		Negative		Interrogative
Long form	**Short form**	**Long form**	**Short form**	
I have got	I've got	I have not got	I haven't got	Have I got?
You have got	You've got	You have not got	You haven't got	Have you got?
He **has** got	He's got	He **has not** got	He **hasn't** got	**Has** he got?
She **has** got	She's got	She **has not** got	She **hasn't** got	**Has** she got?
It **has** got	It's got	It **has not** got	It **hasn't** got	**Has** it got?
We have got	We've got	We have not got	We haven't got	Have we got?
You have got	You've got	You have not got	You haven't got	Have you got?
They have got	They've got	They have not got	They haven't got	Have they got?

(41) **Fill in the blanks as in the example:**

Long form

1. I .....*have got* .... a book.
2. Mary .... a red dress.
3. They .... a dog.
4. It .... big ears.
5. Pam ...*has not got* .... a watch.
6. We .... a telephone.
7. Jane .... a banana.
8. You .... a hat.

Short form

I.....*'ve got*............................ a book.
Mary .... a red dress.
They .... a dog.
It .... big ears.
Pam ....*hasn't got*................. a watch.
We .... a telephone.
Jane .... a banana.
You .... a hat.

42 **Write what these people have got.**

Jill is tall and thin.

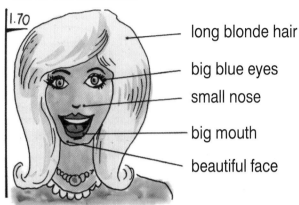

long blonde hair

big blue eyes

small nose

big mouth

beautiful face

Tom is short and fat.

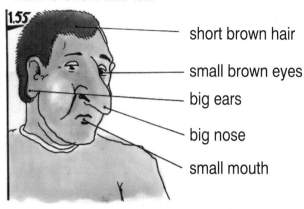

short brown hair

small brown eyes

big ears

big nose

small mouth

Jill *...is tall and thin. She has got long blonde hair. She has got big blue eyes.* ....

....

Tom ....

....

....

43 **Look at the red monster and write about it.**

head

eye

hand

arm

leg

foot

....It has got three eyes. ....

....

....

....

....

....

....

Write about you now.

I have got two hands. ....

....

....

Short answers

Have you got a pen?	**Yes, I / we have.**	**No, I / we haven't.**
Has he / she / it got two pens?	**Yes, he / she / it has.**	**No, he / she / it hasn't.**

8. "Have (got)"

(44) **Ask and answer each other as in the example:**

...Have you got a Walkman?.   *...No, I haven't....*
...Have you got a TV?........   *...Yes, I have. ..*

a Walkman ✗   a TV ✔   a watch ☐   a doll ☐   an umbrella ☐

a yacht ☐   a balloon ☐   a skirt ☐   a ball ☐   a bike ☐

(45) **Fill in "have" or "has", then ask and answer as in the example:**

1. *..Have......* the green monsters got two eyes?   *...Yes, they have.* ....
2. .... the blue monster got two legs? ....
3. .... the red monster got two arms? ....
4. .... the pink monsters got three eyes? ....
5. .... the yellow monster got a big mouth? ....
6. .... the brown monster got two legs? ....

46 Find the differences in picture B.

..Paul has got a red T-shirt. He hasn't got a watch. ....

....

....

....

....

Game 11

The leader writes the name of a girl or boy from the class on a piece of paper. The teams in turn ask questions about his/her eyes, hair, mouth, colours of clothes and shoes to find out who he/she is.

Teacher:	Is it a girl or a boy?		Team A P2:	Has he got brown hair?
Leader:	It's a boy. (George)		Leader:	Yes, he has.
Team A P1:	Has he got brown eyes?		Team B P2:	Has he got brown shoes?
Leader:	No, he hasn't.		Leader:	Yes, he has.
Team B P1:	Has he got blue eyes?		Team A P3:	Is it George?
Leader:	Yes, he has.		Leader:	Yes, it is. (Team A wins)

Writing Activity 2

The police want this purple monster. Describe it.

....

....

....

....

....

9. There is - There are

There is an octopus.
There are three fish.
There are four tins
and five bottles.
There is a diver.
The diver is sad because
people make the sea dirty.

	Affirmative		Negative		Interrogative
	Long form	**Short form**	**Long form**	**Short form**	
singular	there is	there's	there is not	there isn't	Is there?
plural	there are		there are not	there aren't	Are there?

47 First say then write sentences as in the example:

1. house
2. tree
3. window
4. door
5. cat
6. boy
7. woman
8. man
9. dog

1. *..There is a house.*....................
2. ....
3. ....
4. ....
5. ....
6. ....
7. ....
8. ....
9. ....

48 There are four rooms in this house: a kitchen, a living-room, a bedroom and a bathroom. Say what there is in each room.

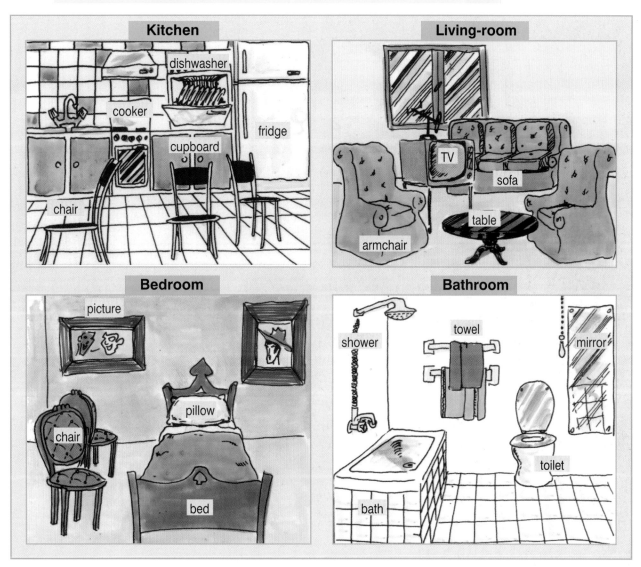

49 Answer the questions as in the example:

1. Is there a fridge in the living-room? *...No, there isn't.*.................................
2. Are there two armchairs in the living-room? ....
3. Is there a sofa in the living-room? ....
4. Are there two towels in the bedroom? ....
5. Is there a cooker in the kitchen? ....

50 Ask each other questions and answer them, then write them.

...Is there a bed in the bathroom? No, there isn't. ....
....
....

9. There is - There are

(51) **Find the differences in picture B.**

1. *...There is a big farmhouse.* ....
2. ....
3. ....
4. ....
5. ....
6. ....
7. ....
8. ....
9. ....
10. ....

 Game 12

Pupils look at the four rooms of the house on page 33 Ex. 48 for 2 - 3 minutes. Then the teams in turn, with books closed, say what there is in the rooms.

　　Team A P1:　　There are three chairs in the kitchen.
　　Team B P1:　　There is a pillow in the bedroom.　　etc

Writing Activity 3

Write what there is in your bedroom.

10. "Can"

I can walk and
I can talk.

I can't fly and
I can't cry.

Can you sing
and can you dance?

I can clap my
hands!!!

Affirmative	Negative		Interrogative
	Long form	**Short form**	
I can	I cannot	I can't	Can I?
You can	You cannot	You can't	Can you?
He can	He cannot	He can't	Can he?
She can	She cannot	She can't	Can she?
It can	It cannot	It can't	Can it?
We can	We cannot	We can't	Can we?
You can	You cannot	You can't	Can you?
They can	They cannot	They can't	Can they?

Short answers	Can you dance?	Yes, I can. / No, I can't.

52 **Answer the questions as in the example:**

1. Can you see a van? ...*No, I can't.* ....
2. Can you see a man? ....
3. Can you see a bed? ....
4. Can you see a boy? ....
5. Can you see a dog? ....
6. Can you see a glass? ....

53 **What can you do? Look at the pictures and tick.**

Then say what you can or can't do.

1. paint ☐   2. sing ☐   3. swim ☐   4. dive ☐

5. read ☐   6. write ☐   7. walk ☐   8. run ☐

9. jump ☐   10. cook ☐   11. clean ☐   12. wash ☐

13. ride ☐   14. drive ☐   15. play tennis ☐   16. climb ☐

17. eat ☐   18. drink ☐   19. see ☐   20. hear ☐

 Game 13

Pupils look at the pictures for Ex. 53 for 2 minutes. Then they close their books and, in teams, say and mime as many verbs as possible.

Team A P1: drive (he mimes driving) | Team B P1: swim (she mimes swimming) etc

54 **Ask and answer questions as in the example:**

1. *...Can Tom dive? No, he can't.* ....
2. ....
3. ....
4. ....
5. ....
6. ....
7. ....
8. ....

55 **True or False?**

1. Fish can swim.   *..True! Fish can swim.* ....
2. Sharks can walk.   ....
3. Babies can cook.   ....
4. Kangaroos can jump.   ....
5. Elephants can drive.   ....
6. Birds can fly.   ....

10. "Can"

Game 14

Pupils read about the monkeys and spot the mistakes. Then the teams in turn correct the mistakes.

Monkeys can walk. **They can sing.** They can't play tennis. They can eat bananas. They can't drink water. They can fly. They can't climb. They can read. They can't write. They can't cook. They can drive. They can run. They can't jump. They are big animals. They've got five legs. They're blue. They've got three eyes.

Team A P1:   Wrong! Monkeys can't sing.   etc

Writing Activity 4

Write what these animals can or can't do.

Birds can fly. They can't write. ....

....

....

....

Revision Exercises II

56 **Fill in: have, has, is, are or can.**

Jim 1) ..*has*.. got black hair and brown eyes. He 2) ....
twenty-two. He 3) .... a student. He 4) ....
swim and play tennis. Jenny and Rosa 5) .... got
brown hair and blue eyes. They 6) .... twelve.
They 7) .... pupils. They 8) .... sing and
dance.

57 **Fill in: he, she, it or they.**

1. John   ..*he*..........   4. horses   ....
2. table   ....   5. Sam and Pam   ....
3. boys   ....   6. Ann   ....

58 **Write the plural form.**

1. lady   ..*ladies*......   6. glass   ....
2. witch   ....   7. child   ....
3. fox   ....   8. hat   ....
4. goose   ....   9. foot   ....
5. boy   ....   10. sheep   ....

59 **Fill in can or can't and the appropriate verb.**

Julie 1) ..*can swim*........   but she 2) ....

She 3) ....   but she 4) ....

She 5) ....   but she 6) ....

She 7) ....   but she 8) ....

Revision Exercises II

(60) **Match the numbers with the words.**

10   sixty   20   twelve   nine   forty   9

twenty

17   13   one

ten   15   60   seventeen   3

eighteen

fifteen   12   three

eight   18

8   thirteen   1   40

(61) **Write short answers.**

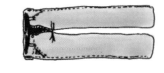

jacket ✓   blouse ✗   scarf ✓   jeans ✓

helmet ✗   slippers ✗   orange dress ✗   brown belt ✗

jumper ✓   tie ✓   shorts ✓   T-shirt ✓

1. Have you got a jacket?   *...Yes, I have.*...
2. Have you got a blouse?   ....
3. Have you got a scarf?   ....
4. Have you got jeans?   ....
5. Have you got a helmet?   ....
6. Have you got slippers?   ....
7. Have you got an orange dress?   ....
8. Have you got a brown belt?   ....
9. Have you got a jumper?   ....
10. Have you got a tie?   ....
11. Have you got shorts?   ....
12. Have you got a T-shirt?   ....

62 Write what there is in the kitchen.

1. ..*There is a fridge.*..............................
2. ....
3. ....
4. ....
5. ....
6. ....

63 Fill in: this, that, these or those.

1. .....*This*.... is  an apple and ...*that*........ is  an orange.

2. .... are  lemons and .... are  grapes.

3. .... is  a melon and .... is  a watermelon.

4. .... are  cherries and .... are  strawberries.

5. .... are  pineapples and .... are  pears.

6. .... are  tomatoes and .... are  carrots.

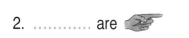

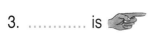

64 **Write what these people have got.**

George
short black hair
big brown eyes
big nose
small mouth
small ears

Jenny
long brown hair
big blue eyes
small nose
big mouth
small ears

George *has got short black hair.*...

....

....

Jenny ....

....

....

65 **Find the mistakes and correct them.**

1. H~~ave~~ he got a Walkman?   *..Has he got a Walkman?* .....
2. There are two mouse.   ....
3. This are snakes.   ....
4. "Has she got a cat?" "No, she isn't." ....
5. I've got two glass.   ....
6. Are there a sofa in the room?   ....
7. It have got two hands.   ....
8. Those is a monkey.   ....
9. Kate have got small ears.   ....
10. This is a umbrella.   ....

66 **True or False?**

1. Dolphins can dance.   *...False! Dolphins can't dance.*..............................
2. Tigers can fly.   ....
3. Sharks can swim.   ....
4. Birds can drive.   ....
5. Monkeys can jump.   ....
6. Goats can sing.   ....
7. Fish can walk.   ....
8. Cats can climb.   ....

11. Possessives

Personal Pronouns		Possessive adjectives	
Singular	**Plural**	**Singular**	**Plural**
I	we	my	our
you	you	your	your
he, she, it	they	his, her, its	their

67 Fill in: my, your, his, her, its, our or their.

1. I've got a scarf.
It's *my* scarf.

2. He's got a jacket.
It's .... jacket.

3. She's got a video camera.
It's .... video camera.

4. They've got sunglasses.
They're .... sunglasses.

5. You've got a computer.
It's .... computer.

6. We've got shorts.
They're .... shorts.

7. It's got a tail.
It's .... tail.

8. They've got T-shirts.
They're ....T-shirts.

9. She's got a schoolbag.
It's .... schoolbag.

Possessive case

This is the boy's ball.

These are the boys' balls.

68 **Read the text then explain the highlighted words.**

I'm Tina. Elsa is my grandma and David is my grandpa. Bob is my father and Kate is my mother. Roy is my brother. I am his sister. Mary is my aunt and Tom is my uncle. Jean and Alice are my cousins. Jean and Alice are sisters. They are Tom and Mary's daughters. Roy is Bob and Kate's son. Elsa is David's wife and David is Elsa's husband. Roy, Jean, Alice and I are Elsa and David's grandchildren.

(69) Underline the possessive case.

Elsa is <u>David's</u> wife. Kate is Bob's wife and Mary is Tom's wife. David is Elsa's husband. Bob is Kate's husband and Tom is Mary's husband. Elsa is Bob's mother. She is Mary's mother, too. Kate is Roy's mother. She is Tina's mother, too. Mary is Jean's mother. She is Alice's mother, too. Bob is Roy's father. He is Tina's father, too. Tom is Jean's father. He is Alice's father, too. Kate is Jean's aunt. She is Alice's aunt, too. Bob is Jean's uncle. He is Alice's uncle, too.

(70) Look at the family tree. Ask and answer questions in pairs.

…*Whose father is David? Bob and Mary's.* ……………………………………………………

………………………………………………………………………………………………………

(71) Look at the family tree and fill in the missing words.

Alice is Jean's 1) ..*sister*.. . Elsa is her 2) …………… and David is her 3) ………… . Mary is Tom's 4) ………… . Bob is Mary's 5) ………… . Jean is Roy's 6) ………… . Kate is Jean's 7) ………… and Bob is Jean's 8) ………… . Alice is Tom's 9) ………… . Bob is Elsa's 10) ………… . Jean and Alice are Elsa's 11) ………… . Tom is Jean's 12) ………… .

(72) Fill in the missing names in the possessive case.

Mary is 1) ..*Tom's*.. wife. David is 2) ………… husband. Tom is 3) ………… and …………… father. Roy is 4) ………… brother. David is 5) ………… grandpa. Bob is 6) ………… son and Mary is 7) ………… daughter.

(73) Fill in: his, her or their.

Bob is Kate's husband. He is 1) ..*her*.. husband. Mary is Tom's wife. She is 2) ……… wife. Jean is Roy and Tina's cousin. She is 3) …………… cousin. Tom is Roy's uncle. He is 4) ……… uncle. Alice is Jean's sister. She is 5) …… sister. Jean and Alice are Mary and Tom's children. They are 6) ……… children. Bob and Mary are David's children. They are 7) ……… children.

(74) Fill in: my, your, his, her, its, our or their.

1. This is Billy and this is ..*his*.. dog.

2. This is Mary and this is …………… lamb.

3. This is Pam and Ted and this is …………… cat.

11. Possessives

4. This is me and this is .... bike.

5. This is you and this is .... parrot.

6. We are Rob and Kevin and this is .... snake.

7. This is a robot and this is .... head.

8. This is me and this is .... kite.

9. This is Kim and Sam and this is .... rabbit.

Game 15

The teacher says sentences and pupils in teams substitute the names with possessive adjectives. Each correct sentence gets 1 point. The team with the most points is the winner.

Teacher: It's John's car.
Team A P1:   It's **his** car.

Teacher: It's Ann's car.
Team B P1:   It's **her** car.   etc

Writing Activity 5

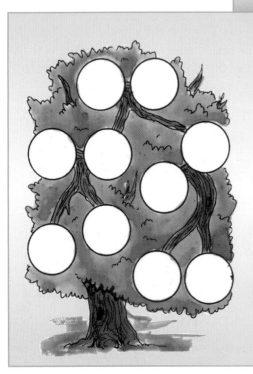

Make your family tree and write a text like the one in Exercise 68.

I'm ....

....

....

....

....

....

....

12. Imperative

We use the imperative to tell one or more people to do or not to do something.

(75) **Match the sentences with the pictures.**

Brush your teeth!   Tidy your room!   Do your homework!
Go to bed!   Drink your milk!   Wake up!

1. *...Wake up!.................*   2. ....   3. ....

4. ....   5. ....   6. ....

12. Imperative

Positive	Negative

(76) Write the negative form.

1. Close your book!   *..Don't close your book!*...
2. Sit on that chair!   ....
3. Run!   ....
4. Look at me!   ....

(77) Fill in the blanks with one of the verbs from the box.

sit, come, open, close, don't climb, don't wake up

1. *.Sit..* down, please!   2. .... the window, please!   3. .... that tree!

4. .... the baby!   5. .... the door, please!   6. .... here, please!

Game 16

Pupils give orders in a chain. The next pupil in the chain mimes the action and gives another order to the next pupil. If a pupil fails to mime the action, he/she is out of the game.

P1:	Jump!	P3:	(mimes singing)	T:	No! P4 is out of the game etc
P2:	(mimes jumping)		Dance!		
	Sing!	P4:	(mimes sleeping)		

13. Present Continuous

Two frogs are standing by,
Two butterflies are flying high,
and to the frogs they're saying goodbye.
He's singing, she's dancing,
they're running, they're jumping,
they're playing in the sun,
they're having fun.

Affirmative		Negative		Interrogative
Long form	**Short form**	**Long form**	**Short form**	
I am walking	I'm walking	I am not walking	I'm not walking	Am I walking?
You are walking	You're walking	You are not walking	You aren't walking	Are you walking?
He is walking	He's walking	He is not walking	He isn't walking	Is he walking?
She is walking	She's walking	She is not walking	She isn't walking	Is she walking?
It is walking	It's walking	It is not walking	It isn't walking	Is it walking?
We are walking	We're walking	We are not walking	We aren't walking	Are we walking?
You are walking	You're walking	You are not walking	You aren't walking	Are you walking?
They are walking	They're walking	They are not walking	They aren't walking	Are they walking?

Spelling rules

work - work**ing**, read - read**ing**   etc
but: <u>cut</u> - cu**tt**ing, sto<u>p</u> - sto**pp**ing, div<u>e</u> - div**ing**, writ<u>e</u> - writ**ing**   etc

We use **Present Continuous** for temporary actions or actions happening now.

(78) Add -ing to the verbs.

1. climb	*..climbing*	4. cook	....	7. dance	....
2. swim	....	5. ride	....	8. write	....
3. cut	....	6. run	....	9. drive	....

13. Present Continuous

(79) Fill in: am, is or are.

1. He ..*is*.. eating a banana.
2. It .... flying.
3. I .... reading.
4. They .... dancing.
5. She .... cooking.
6. We .... walking.

(80) Complete the sentences as in the example:

Long form	Short form
1. I ..*am*... singing.	I ..*'m*... singing.
2. We .... brushing our teeth.	We .... brushing our teeth.
3. He .... doing his homework.	He .... doing his homework.
4. It .... flying.	It .... flying.
5. They ...*are not*.. drinking tea.	They ..*aren't*.. drinking tea.
6. You .... sitting.	You .... sitting.
7. She .... swimming.	She .... swimming.
8. It .... barking.	It .... barking.

(81) Read the text and write the people's names in the picture.
Then cover the text and say what the people are doing.

Pam is reading a book. Ben and Helen are sitting in the sun. Paul is kicking a ball. Mike is drinking Coke. Jenny is crying. Carol is eating an ice-cream. Jane and Susan are singing. Steven and Alice are listening to the radio . Harry is sleeping. George is painting. Mary is brushing her hair.

Now ask questions based on the text above.

...*Is Pam reading a book?*... etc

82 Fill in the blanks with Present Continuous.

The prince 1) ..*is looking*... (look) at the water. A swan 2) .... (swim).
Birds 3) .... (fly) in the sky. The prince's horse 4) .... (eat)
grass. Bob and Tim 5) .... (sit) on a rock. They 6) .... (talk).
Look! The prince 7) .... (cry). Can you guess why?

Short answers

Are you/they reading?	Yes, I am /we /they are.	Is he/she/it reading?	Yes, he /she /it is.
	No, I'm not /we /they aren't.		No, he /she /it isn't.

83 Look at the picture above and answer as in the example:

1. Is the prince swimming?   ....*No, he isn't.* ....
2. Is the swan flying? ....
3. Are the birds swimming? ....
4. Is the prince crying? ....
5. Are Bob and Tim playing? ....
6. Is the prince's horse eating grass? ....

Game 17

Pupils look at picture for Ex. 81. The teacher chooses a leader and asks him/her to think of a person in
the picture. Pupils in teams try to guess who the person is.

Leader:	He's a boy. (Harry)	Team A P2:	Is he sleeping?
Team A P1:	Is he painting?	Leader:	Yes, he is.
Leader:	No, he isn't.	Team A P2:	He's Harry.
Team B P1:	Is he diving?	Leader:	Yes, he is.
Leader:	No, he isn't.		Team A wins.

84 Read the text then find the mistakes and correct them as in the example:

Flog · Zog · Bob · Flig · Alice · Pog · Don · Blog

Zog is swimming. Blog is singing. Alice and Bob are jumping. Don is reading. Flog and Flig are crying. Pog is eating grass.

1. ..Zog isn't swimming. He's eating. ....
2. ....
3. ....
4. ....
5. ....
6. ....

85 Find the differences and write sentences as in the example:

A · B

..In picture A the wolf is looking at Little Red Riding Hood. ....
..In picture B the wolf isn't looking at Little Red Riding Hood. He's sleeping. ....
..In picture A the birds ....
....
....
....

Game 18

Pupils in teams look at the pictures for Ex. 85 and ask and answer questions. Each correct question or answer scores 1 point.

Team A P1:   Are the birds in picture A flying?   │   Team B P1:   No, they aren't. They're singing.

Writing Activity 6

Write what they are doing now.

1. Robin Hood ....

2. Marion ....

3. Ben ....

4. Bob and Tim ....

5. The birds ....

6. The dogs ....

7. John ....

8. Paul ....

9. The butterflies ....

10. The frogs ....

14. Present Simple

Do and does, does and do
This is what I usually do
I fish with my net
I feed my little pet
I swim and run
my life is fun.

Affirmative	Negative		Interrogative
	Long form	**Short form**	
I walk	I do not walk	I don't walk	Do I walk?
You walk	You do not walk	You don't walk	Do you walk?
He walk**s**	He **does** not walk	He **doesn't** walk	**Does** he walk?
She walk**s**	She **does** not walk	She **doesn't** walk	**Does** she walk?
It walk**s**	It **does** not walk	It **doesn't** walk	**Does** it walk?
We walk	We do not walk	We don't walk	Do we walk?
You walk	You do not walk	You don't walk	Do you walk?
They walk	They do not walk	They don't walk	Do they walk?

We use Present Simple **for repeated actions or permanent situations.**

Spelling of 3rd person singular for verbs ending in:

ss, sh, ch, x, o + es	consonant + y ➡ ies	vowel + y + s
I kiss - he kiss**es**	I cry - he cr**ies**	I play - he play**s**

(86) Write the 3rd person singular.

1. I swim - he ..*swims*....
2. I study - he ....
3. I pay - he ....
4. I go - he ....
5. I buy - he ....
6. I watch - he ....
7. I fly - he ....
8. I wash - he ....
9. I write - he ....
10. I open - he ....
11. I come - he ....
12. I have - he ....
13. I carry - he ....
14. I make - he ....
15. I walk - he ....

87 **Complete the sentences as in the example:**

Long form	Short form
1. We ...*do not* .... smoke.	We ...*don't*................... smoke.
2. He .... eat fish.	He .... eat fish.
3. She .... watch TV.	She .... watch TV.
4. I .... drive a car.	I ....drive a car.
5. They .... play tennis.	They .... play tennis.
6. Kate .... speak French.	Kate .... speak French.
7. You .... get up at 7.00.	You .... get up at 7.00.

88 **Fill in the blanks with Present Simple.**

Mike 1) ..*is*.. (be) twelve. He 2) ....
.... (have) got blond hair and blue eyes.
Mike 3) .... (like) tennis.
Every Saturday he 4) .... (play)
tennis. His father 5) ....
(cook) him a big breakfast on Saturday
morning. Mike 6) ....
(eat) it and 7) .... (go out)
to play.

89 **Write what they like or they don't like.**

Paul   Coke   pizza   carrots

1. Paul ..*likes Coke and pizza*...................
   ..*He doesn't like carrots.* ....

Sue & Ann   oranges   strawberries   pears

2. Sue and Ann ....
   ....

Jean   fish   meat   potatoes

3. Jean ....
   ....

You   cherries   onions   grapes

4. I ....
   ....

55

14. Present Simple

Short answers

Do you / they like apples?	Yes, I / we / they do.	No, I / we / they don't.
Does he / she / it like apples?	Yes, he / she / it does.	No, he / she / it doesn't.

90 Complete the text with Present Simple, then answer the questions as in the example:

John and David are friends. John 1) .....*likes*....... (like) sports. He 2) .... (swim) every day. John and David 3) .... (play) basketball every week. They don't play tennis. David 4) .... (like) running. John 5) .... (like) books. Every night he 6) .... (read) a story before he 7) .... (go) to bed.

1. Does John like sports? ..*Yes, he does.*.............
2. Does John swim every day? ....
3. Do John and David play tennis? ....
4. Does David like running? ....
5. Does John like books? ....
6. Does John read stories every night? ....

91 Use the verb list and fill in with Present Simple:

get up, ride, take, have got, help, carry

Pete is a postman. He 1) ....*gets up*........ at 5 o'clock. He 2) .... his bike to work. He 3) .... letters to all the houses. Pete 4) .... a dog, Paddy. Paddy 5) .... Pete. He 6) .... the letters in his mouth!

92 Ask questions based on the text above.

..*Is Pete a policeman? Is Pete a postman? Does he get up at 3 o'clock?*   etc ....

....
....
....

Present Simple is used for repeated actions or permanent situations. **Usually, always, often, never, every day** etc are used with Present Simple.	Present Continuous is used for temporary actions or actions happening now. **Now, at present, today, at the moment** etc are used with Present Continuous.
Usually	**Today**
He **usually** drives a car.	**Today** he is riding a bike.

93 **Fill in with Present Simple or Present Continuous.**

1. Mary usually ..*walks*. to school but today she ...*is riding* .... a bike to school.

2. Tom usually .... tennis but today he .... basketball.

3. They usually .... TV but today they .... a party.

4. He usually ....but today he ....

94 **Fill in the blanks with Present Simple or Present Continuous.**

Fred is a fireman. He 1) ...*fights*.... (fight) fires. He 2) .... (drive) a big red fire engine. Can you see him? He 3) .... (put) water onto the fire. He 4) .... (wear) a helmet.

95 **Fill in with Present Simple or Present Continuous.**

USUALLY   AT THE MOMENT

Cinderella usually 1) ..*wears*.. (wear) old clothes. She 2) .... (clean) the house every day and she 3) .... (cook) for her sisters. At night she usually 4) .... (read) a book. At the moment Cinderella 5) .... (wear) a beautiful dress. She 6) .... (dance) with a prince. Cinderella's sisters 7) .... (stand) at the door. They 8) .... (look) at her. They're angry.

96 **Fill in with Present Simple or Present Continuous.**

Sarah Star is a singer. She 1) ....*sings*..... (sing) and 2) .... (dance) on TV. She 3) .... (drive) a red Mercedes. At the moment she is with Nick Pear. They 4) .... (eat) in a restaurant. Sarah 5) .... (drink) Cola and Nick 6) .... (talk) to the waiter.

97 **Put the verbs in the correct tense.**

1. a) I usually ......*drink*........ (drink) tea.
    b) Today I ..*'m drinking*........... (drink) coffee.
2. a) I usually .... (eat) lunch at one o'clock.
    b) Today I .... (eat) at twelve o'clock.
3. a) She .... (visit) her grandmother now.
    b) She .... (visit) her grandmother every week.

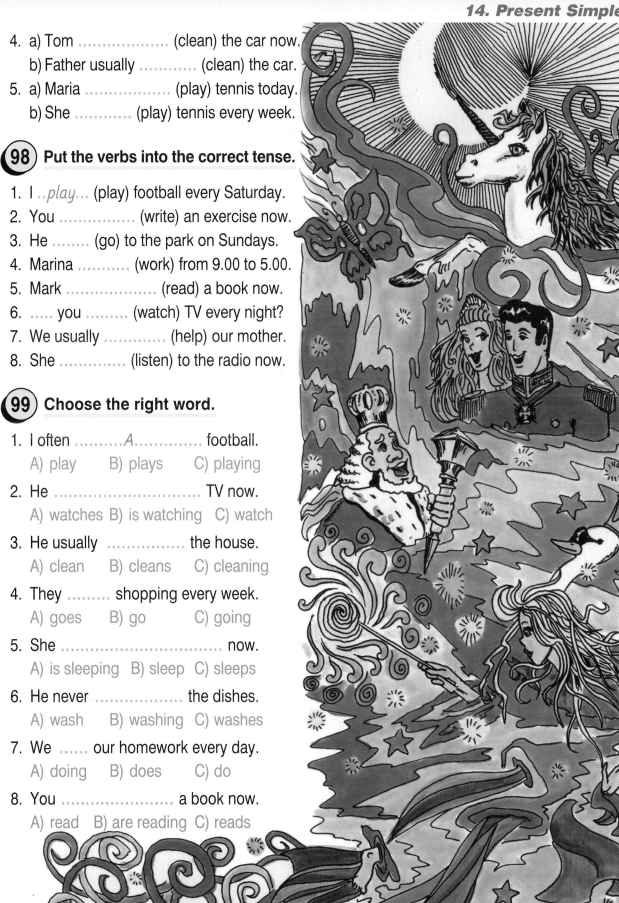

4. a) Tom .... (clean) the car now.
   b) Father usually .... (clean) the car.
5. a) Maria .... (play) tennis today.
   b) She .... (play) tennis every week.

98 **Put the verbs into the correct tense.**

1. I ..*play*... (play) football every Saturday.
2. You .... (write) an exercise now.
3. He .... (go) to the park on Sundays.
4. Marina .... (work) from 9.00 to 5.00.
5. Mark .... (read) a book now.
6. ..... you .... (watch) TV every night?
7. We usually .... (help) our mother.
8. She .... (listen) to the radio now.

99 **Choose the right word.**

1. I often ....*A*.............. football.
   A) play   B) plays   C) playing
2. He .... TV now.
   A) watches B) is watching C) watch
3. He usually .... the house.
   A) clean   B) cleans   C) cleaning
4. They .... shopping every week.
   A) goes   B) go   C) going
5. She .... now.
   A) is sleeping B) sleep C) sleeps
6. He never .... the dishes.
   A) wash   B) washing C) washes
7. We ...... our homework every day.
   A) doing   B) does   C) do
8. You .... a book now.
   A) read   B) are reading C) reads

(100) **Write what Carol does every day.**

Carol 1) ....*gets up*...... at 7 o'clock every day. She 2) .... breakfast at 7.30. She 3) .... to school at 8 o'clock. She 4) .... lunch at 2 o'clock. She 5) .... her homework in the evening. She 6) .... TV at 8 o'clock. She 7) .... to bed at 10 o'clock.

Game 19

Pupils in teams say sentences using the verbs in the list below in Present Simple. Each correct sentence scores 1 point. Negations or questions get 2 points each if they're correct.

Verb list: **swims, write letters, goes, do homework, read, play, makes tea, watch TV, gets up, cooks, washes, walk, works, plays**

Team A P1: My brother **swims** every week. | Team B P1: Do you usually **write letters** to friends?

Writing Activity 7

Write about you. What do you do every day at 7 o'clock, 7.30, 8.30, 1.30, 5 o'clock, 9 o'clock?

..I get up at 7 o'clock. I wash my face and brush my teeth. At 7.30 I ....

....

....

....

....

Revision Exercises III

101 **Look at the pictures then write about picture B.**

1. There is a butterfly.
2. There is a girl.
3. The girl has got a ball.
4. A boy is swimming.
5. A woman is in the garden.
6. A man is sitting on a chair.
7. The man has got a newspaper.

..There are three butterflies..................
....
....
....
....
....
....

102 **Rewrite the text changing the underlined words as in the example:**

Today is <u>Tom's</u> birthday. <u>Tom</u> is in the garden. <u>Tom's</u> friends are in the garden, too. <u>Tom's friends</u> are playing. Tom's mother is coming. Look at <u>Mother's</u> dress! <u>Tom's mother</u> is bringing a birthday cake. <u>The birthday cake</u> has got ten candles on it. <u>Tom's</u> father is coming, too. <u>Tom's father</u> is holding a camera. *...Today is his birthday. ....*

103 **Write what there is in the picture.**

1. *..There is a farmhouse...........................*
2. ....
3. ....
4. ....
5. ....
6. ....
7. ....

61

Revision Exercises III

104 **Fill in the blanks with one of the verbs from the box.**

stand	open	drink	sit	read	eat

1. ..*Drink*............ your milk! 2. .... on the chair! 3. .... the window, please!

4. .... your chicken! 5. .... up! 6. .... this book!

105 **Fill in: have, has, is, are, am or can.**

Hello! I 1) ... *am* ... Julie Smith. I 2) .... got two brothers, Jim and Ted. They 3) .... sixteen years old. Jim 4) .... a student. He 5) .... swim and dive. Ted 6) .... got a bike. He likes riding it.

106 **Fill in: this, that, these or those.**

1. ..*This*....... is 🖝 a ball and .... is 🖝 a doll.

2. .... are 🖝 rabbits and .... are 🖝 foxes.

3. .... is 🖝 a star and .... is 🖝 a yacht.

4. .... are 🖝 pens and .... are 🖝 books.

107 **Read the text then answer the questions.**

Hi! My name is Sue. I live in this house. I can ride a bike but I can't drive. I like swimming but I don't like dancing. I'm swimming now. I've got two cats. They don't like swimming.

1. Is her name Sue? *..Yes, it is.* ....
2. Does she live in this house? ....
3. Can she drive? ....
4. Can she ride a bike? ....
5. Does she like dancing? ....

6. Is she climbing now? ....
7. Is she swimming now? ....
8. Has she got three cats? ....
9. Do her cats like swimming? ....

108 **Fill in with Present Continuous.**

This is Willy the penguin. Look at him! He 1) *..is diving..* (dive). He has got

a fish and he 2) .... (eat) it. He 3) .... (look)

at Monica, a beautiful penguin. He 4) .... (dance) for her.

He 5) .... (sing) for her, too. Look! He 6) .... (run)

to her! Oh! They 7) .... (dance).

(109) **Fill in with Present Simple.**

Dear Mary,

My name 1) ...*is*.. (be) Sally. I 2) .... (be) ten years old and I

3) .... (come) from England. I 4) .... (have) got a big family. We

5) .... (live) in a big house. My father 6) .... (work) in a

bank. My mother 7) .... (not/work) in a bank, she 8) ....

(work) in a hospital. She 9) .... (do) the x-rays. My two brothers

10) .... (go) to school in the morning. My sister Tina 11) ....

(stay) at home. She 12) .... (be) two years old. I

13) .... (have) got a pet dog, Johnny. We 14) ....

(love) him very much. Write to me soon.

Love,

Sally

(110) **Fill in with Present Simple or Present Continuous.**

Boy: What 1) *are you doing* (you/do) here?
Girl: I 2) .... (wash) my clothes.
    I usually 3) .... (swim) but
    today I 4) .... (do) my
    washing. Oh! Look at the monkeys!
Boy: They usually 5) .... (climb) the
    trees but today they 6) ....
    (eat) bananas.
Girl: Yes. They 7) .... (be) very
    happy.

(111) **Fill in with Present Simple or Present Continuous.**

This 1) ....*is*...... (be) a sea monster. It
2) .... (eat) fish and ships.
Look! It 3) .... (swim).
It 4) .... (go) to the boat.
Oh no! There 5) .... (be)
two people in the boat. They cannot see
the sea monster. The man 6) ....
.... (dive) into the water.

(112) Fill in the blanks as in the example:

USUALLY 6 o'clock in the evening   TODAY 6 o'clock in the evening

1. Ann usually ....*reads*........... but today she ......*is watching*.......................... TV.
2. Dad usually .... dinner but today he .... to the radio.
3. Mum usually .... the newspaper but today she .... to the radio.
4. The children usually .... their homework but today they ....

(113) Choose the correct item.

1. He never .... *C* .... old cars.
   A) drive   B) driving   C) drives

2. This is Tom and this is .... mum.
   A) her   B) his   C) he

3. "Have you got a pet?" "Yes, ..."
   A) have   B) I have   C) have I

4. She .... at 7.30 every day.
   A) gets up   B) get up   C) getting up

5. These are the .... dolls.
   A) girls   B) girls'   C) girl

6. .... to bed!
   A) Goes   B) Doesn't go C) Go

(114) Find the mistakes and correct them.

1. She don't like fish.   ..*She doesn't like fish.*......
2. Have Ann got a cat?   ....
3. She swimming now.   ....
4. This is a onion.   ....
5. These is apples.   ....
6. Does he plays tennis?   ....
7. Is Ben and Tom dancing?   ....
8. Tony and Mary hasn't got a dog. ....
9. They sleeping.   ....
10. This is Anns skirt.   ....
11. It has got two foot.   ....
12. Sally don't work.   ....

15. Prepositions of place

115 Fill in: on, in, under or behind.

1. ..*in* .... 2. .... 3. .... 4. ....

116 Fill in: in, on, behind or under.

Beauty is 1) ..*in*... the room. The Beast is 2) .... her. There's a picture 3) .... the wall. There's a table 4) .... the picture. There's a rose 5) .... the glass case 6) .... the table. Beauty is looking at the rose.

(117) Fill in: **in, on, behind or under.**

Cinderella is sitting 1) ...*on*.. a chair. The prince has got a shoe 2) .... his hand. Her sisters are 3) .... her. They are looking at Cinderella and the prince. There's a mouse 4) .... the table. It is smiling. Who's the mouse? Can you guess?

(118) Fill in: **in, on, behind or under.**

The red monster is 1) ..*on*.. the fridge. It's drinking milk. The yellow and the purple monsters are 2) .... the fridge. They are eating jam. The green monster is 3) .... the door. The orange monster is 4) .... the table. It's eating a cake.

119 Fill in: on, in, under or behind.

The fox is 1) ..*in*.. the room. The white hen is 2) .... the bed. The black hen is 3) .... the sofa. The brown hen is 4) .... the wardrobe. The fox is hungry. It wants to eat the little hens. Look! Mrs Smith is 5) .... the fox. She's wearing a hat 6) .... her head. She's holding an umbrella 7) .... her hand. She is very angry.

Game 20

Where's the treasure: under the boat, behind the boat, in the cave, on the rocks, under the rocks, in the birds' nest, behind the birds' nest, under the birds' nest, in the tree?

The leader hides the treasure in one of the above places. Pupils in teams try to guess where the treasure is. The first team to find the treasure is the winner.

Leader:	(treasure under the boat)		Team B P1:	Is it under the birds' nest?
Team A P1:	Is it in the tree?		Leader:	No, it isn't. etc
Leader:	No, it isn't.			

Writing Activity 8

Look at the picture and answer the questions.

Where are the shirts? ....
Where are the trousers? ....
Where are the shoes? ....
Where's the table? ....
Where's the vase? ....
Where are the flowers? ....
Where's the picture? ....
Where's the cat? ....

16. Prepositions of time

> In the morning I wash my face.
> In the evening I clean the place.
> At 2 o'clock I watch TV.
> At 5 o'clock I swim in the sea.
> On Wednesdays I go to school.
> On Sundays I go to the pool.

IN	AT	ON
in the morning	at 8 o'clock	on Sunday, on Monday,
in the afternoon	at Eid	on Tuesday, on Wednesday,
in the evening	at night	on Thursday, on Friday,
in July (months)	at midnight	on Saturday, on August 2nd,
in summer (seasons)	at Easter	on Christmas Day
in 1991 (years)	at the weekend	

120 **Match the pictures with the seasons:** summer, winter, spring, autumn.

December, January, February

March, April, May

June, July, August

September, October, November

16. Prepositions of time

121 Fill in: on, in or at.

Come to my party
..on... Monday
.... 4 o'clock
.... the afternoon.

122 Fill in: in, on or at.

1. ...in.. December
2. .... Friday
3. ..... the weekend
4. .... winter
5. ..... the morning
6. 1991

7. .... 4 o'clock
8. .... night
9. .... 11 o'clock
10. .... August
11. .... summer
12. .... Sunday

123 Underline the correct preposition.

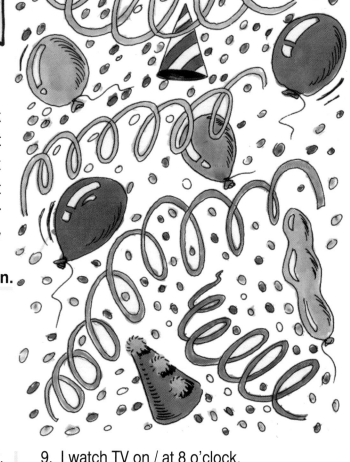

1. I get up at / in 7.30.
2. August is in / on summer.
3. It rains in / at January.
4. I go to the park on / in the afternoon.
5. She goes to the gym at / on Tuesdays.
6. We play tennis in / on the morning.
7. We have chocolate eggs at / on Easter.
8. We play football on / in Fridays.
9. I watch TV on / at 8 o'clock.
10. We sleep at / in night.

124 Rewrite the words in the box adding on, in or at.

8 o'clock	Monday	Easter	spring
Christmas	winter	Tuesday	the morning
March 1st	the weekend	7 o'clock	Eid	night

..at 8 o'clock, in winter ....
....
....

125 Fill in: in, on or at.

Sylvester gets up 1) *at* 6 o'clock. He eats eggs 2) .... Mondays and Wednesdays but he drinks only milk 3) .... Tuesdays, Thursdays, Fridays, Saturdays and Sundays. He goes to the gym 4) .... 8 o'clock 5) .... the morning. He eats lunch 6) .... 2 o'clock 7) .... the afternoon. He swims 8) .... the afternoon. He goes to bed early 9) .... night.

126 What does Sally do on Mondays?

seven o'clock   half past eight   quarter to three   quarter past nine

..Sally gets up at seven o'clock. ....

....

Now write what you do on Tuesdays.

....

....

127 Choose the correct item.

1. I go to school .....*A*.......... the morning.
   A) in   B) on   C) at

2. Dad comes home .... half past six.
   A) on   B) at   C) in

3. .... Sunday we go to the beach.
   A) At   B) In   C) On

4. We give presents .... Christmas.
   A) in   B) on   C) at

5. It rains .... winter.
   A) on   B) in   C) at

6. My birthday is .... November 9th.
   A) on   B) at   C) in

7. She doesn't work .... night.
   A) at   B) in   C) on

8. We have lunch .... twelve o'clock.
   A) in   B) on   C) at

9. I watch TV .... the evening.
   A) at   B) in   C) on

10. School starts .... September.
    A) at   B) on   C) in

16. Prepositions of time

(128) Fill in: on, in or at.

Ben Walker is a farmer. He gets up 1) .at.. 5 o'clock 2) .... the morning. He has breakfast 3) .... half past five, then he goes to the farm. He comes back home 4) .... noon. 5) ...... the afternoon he meets his friends. 6) ... Sundays he stays at home and watches TV.

(129) Fill in: in, on or at.

Dear Jessica,

My birthday party is 1) ..on... August 2nd. Can you come? The party is 2) .... 7 o'clock 3) .... the evening. You can come 4) .... the morning. The party is 5) ....
Saturday.

Love,
Nina

Game 21

The teacher divides the class into two teams and says time expressions. Each team in turn adds the correct preposition. Each correct answer gets 1 point. The team with the most points is the winner.

Teacher:	December		Teacher:	Christmas
Team A P1:	in December		Team B P1:	at Christmas etc

Writing Activity 9

Write an invitation card to your friend. Use Ex. 121 as a model.

17. Who - What

Who is used for people. What is used for things and animals.

130 Match up the sentences.

1. Who is she?	A. It is a book.	1. ....*D*....................
2. What is this?	B. He is sleeping.	2. ....
3. What are those?	C. They are John and Mary.	3. ....
4. Who are they?	D. She is Ann.	4. ....
5. What is he doing?	E. They are fish.	5. ....

131 Fill in: who or what.

1. *What* is that?

It's a dragon.

2. .... are they?

They're my friends.

3. .... is that?

GGGRR!

It's a bear. Run!

73

17. Who – What

(132) Fill in: who or what.

1. *What*...... are those?
They're penguins.

2. .... is she?
She's Sarah.

3. .... are they?
They're Tom and Kim.

4. .... is that?
It's a hat.

5. .... is this?
It's a robot.

6. .... is he?
He's my father.

(133) Fill in "who" or "what", then answer the questions.

1. ...*Who*........ is the bear? ....*Peter*.. . ...*What* .... has he got? A banana.
2. .... is the pirate? .... has he got? A sword.
3. .... has the ballerina got? A flower. .... is the ballerina? ....
4. .... are the ghosts? .... are the robots? ....
5. .... has Dracula got? Big teeth. .... has the doctor got? A bag.
6. .... have the robots got? Balloons. .... is the doctor? ....
7. .... has the cowboy got? A big hat. .... is the cowboy? ....
8. .... have the ghosts got? White gloves. .... is Dracula? ....

74

134 Fill in: who or what.

Bob: Hello. Can you hear me?

Prof. Jones: Yes. 1) ..*Who*... is that?

Bob: It's Bob. 2) .... are you?

Prof. Jones: I'm Professor Jones. 3) ....
can you see?

Bob: I can see lots of flowers.

Prof. Jones: 4) .... colour are they?

Bob: Yellow. And there are blue fruit trees.

Prof. Jones: 5) .... is in the tree?

Bob: It's a green monster.

Prof. Jones: 6) .... has it got?

Bob: It's got a blue fruit.

Game 22

This is a picture of a school play. Teams in turn ask questions using **who** or **what**. Each correct answer gets 1 point. The team with the most points is the winner.

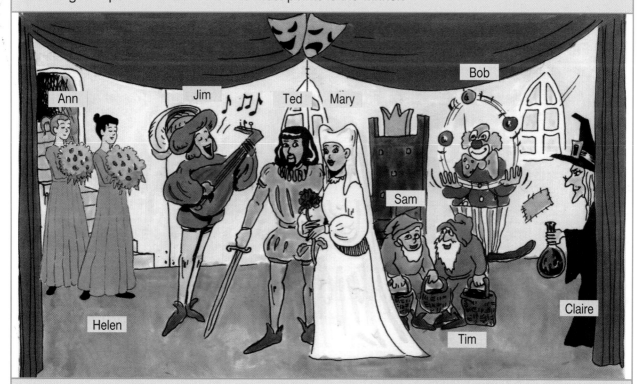

Team A P1: **Who**'s the prince?	Team A P2: He's got a sword.
Team B P1: It's Ted. **What** has he got?	**Who**'s the princess? etc

Revision Exercises IV

(135) Fill in: in, on, under or behind.

There are three boys 1) ..*in*.. the picture. Johnny is 2) .... a tree. He is sleeping. Timmy is 3) .... a branch. He is watching the birds. Tommy is chasing butterflies. Tommy's dog is 4) .... him.

(136) Fill in: on, in or at.

Dear Sam,

I am from Italy. I am twelve years old. My birthday is 1) ..*on*... July 13th. I get up 2) .... 7 o'clock every day. 3) .... Tuesdays I go to the pool. 4) .... the summer I usually go camping. 5) .... Christmas we go skiing. Write to me soon.

Yours,

Nicola

(137) Fill in: this, these, that or those.

1. ...*This*........ is 👉 a girl and ...*that* .... is 👉 a boy.

2. .... are 👉 onions and .... are 👉 tomatoes.

3. .... is 👉 a book and .... is 👉 a pen.

(138) Write what there is in the picture.

1. ..*There are two boys.*.................................
2. ....
3. ....
4. ....

(139) Fill in: who or what.

Bobby: 1) ...*Who*..'s that?

  Tina: She's my friend, Mary.

Bobby: 2) .... is she wearing?

  Tina: She's wearing tennis clothes.

Bobby: And 3) .... 's that in her hand?

  Tina: It's a racquet. She's playing tennis.

Bobby: 4) .... 's she playing with?

  Tina: She's playing with John.

Bobby: 5) .... 's John?

  Tina: He's her brother! Please stop asking questions!

(140) Fill in with Present Simple or Present Continuous.

Hi! I 1) ..*am*.. (be) Susan. I 2) .... (work) in this house. This 3) .... (be) my friend, Tina. She 4) .... (work) here, too. I usually 5) .... (cook) but today I 6) .... (dig) in the garden. Tina usually 7) .... (clean) the house but today she 8) .... (sleep). Wake up, Tina!

(141) Rewrite the text changing the underlined words as in the example:

The Browns are in the park. Tony is sleeping. 1) <u>Tony's</u> sister is wearing a hat. 2) <u>Tony's sister</u> is not eating an ice-cream. 3) <u>Tony's</u> brothers are twins. 4) <u>Tony's brothers</u> are playing with a ball. 5) <u>The ball</u> is red and white. 6) <u>Tony's</u> mother is sitting under a sunshade. 7) <u>Tony's mother</u> is reading a book. 8) <u>Tony's</u> father is having a drink.

The Browns are in the park. Tony is sleeping.

His sister ....

....

....

....

....

(142) Fill in with Present Simple or Present Continuous.

Father: Tom, what 1) *are you doing* (you / do)?

Tom: I 2) .... (clean) the house. I
usually 3) .... (do) my
homework but today I 4) ....
(not / go) to school.

Father: Where's your mum?

Tom: She 5) .... (make) a cake.
She usually 6) .... (go)
to the office but today my friends 7) .... (come) and
we 8) .... (have) a party.

(143) Fill in: have, has, is, are, am or can, then answer with short answers.

My name 1) ..*is*.. Suzie. I 2) .... ten years
old. I 3) .... got one sister and one
brother. My brother 4) .... got a car. He
5) .... drive well but he can't ride a bike. We
6) .... a happy family. We live in a big house.
There 7) .... ten rooms in my house.
Today we 8) .... going on a picnic.

1. Is her name Molly? ...*No, it isn't*.......... .
2. Is she ten years old? ....
3. Has she got two sisters? ....
4. Has she got two brothers? ....

5. Can her brother ride a bike? ....
6. Can he drive? ....
7. Do they live in a big house? ....
8. Are they going to school today? ....

(144) Rewrite the following text in the plural.

He is a pupil. He has got a bike. He can swim and climb. He goes to school every day.
Today he's going out with his friend. ...*They are pupils*. ....

....

(145) Fill in with: sit, tidy or go.

1. .... your room!

2. ....
on that chair, please!

3. .... to bed!

(146) Choose the correct item.

1. "............*C*........ are you?" "I'm John."
   A) Whose   B) What   C) Who

2. She never .... a bike.
   A) ride   B) rides   C) is riding

3. These are the .... shoes.
   A) boys'   B) boy   C) boys

4. .... your face, please!
   A) Washes   B) Wash   C) Doesn't wash

5. .... he play tennis on Sundays?
   A) Does   B) Do   C) Is

6. My birthday is .... October.
   A) on   B) at   C) in

7. Look at those .... !
   A) woman's   B) women   C) woman

8. Greg .... my friend.
   A) is   B) am   C) are

9. .... he like cherries?
   A) Do   B) Does   C) Don't

10. I .... five years old.
    A) are   B) is   C) am

11. This is Ted and this is .... cat.
    A) their   B) his   C) he

12. I go swimming .... Mondays.
    A) at   B) in   C) on

13. "Has he got a TV?" "No, ..."
    A) he has   B) he hasn't   C) has he

14. They .... TV now.
    A) watch   B) watches   C) are watching

15. Look at those .... !
    A) butterflies   B) butterfly   C) butterfly's

16. He .... like carrots.
    A) do   B) doesn't   C) don't

17. She goes to school .... 8.30.
    A) at   B) in   C) on

18. "Is he swimming?" "Yes, ..."
    A) he isn't   B) is he   C) he is

19. She .... swimming.
    A) like   B) likes   C) don't like

20. These are .... hats.
    A) Sally   B) Sallys'   C) Sally's

(147) Find the mistakes and correct them.

1. He ~~don~~'t drink milk.   *..He doesn't drink milk...*
2. January is on winter.   ....
3. John have got a boat.   ....
4. Two woman are in the car.   ....
5. She goes to bed in 8 o'clock.   ....
6. Johns books are on the desk.   ....
7. Do you usually reading?   ....
8. We go skiing on December.   ....
9. He mother is a doctor.   ....
10. She talking to Bob now.   ....
11. Tim and Ted doesn't like apples.   ....

148 **Look at the text, then write questions and answer them.**

Peter is a policeman. He works in a police station. He likes his job. He usually works in the mornings. Today he is working at night. Look! He's chasing a thief.

...Is Peter a mechanic? No, he isn't. Does he work in a police station? Yes, he does.... etc

149 **Read the text, then find the mistakes and correct them as in the example:**

Sally is running. Tim and Joe are swimming. Paula and Jane are dancing. David is drinking Coke. Tom is sleeping. Emma is reading a newspaper.

1. ....*Wrong! Sally isn't running. She's riding her bike.*..................................
2. ....
3. ....
4. ....
5. ....
6. ....

150 **Look at the text, then write questions and answer them.**

Sheila and Jenny are acrobats. They work in a circus. They can walk on a rope. They work at night. Today they aren't working. Sheila is reading. Jenny is cooking.

...Are Sheila and Jenny acrobats? Yes, they are. Do they work in a school? No, they don't.... etc

Pre-Tests

Pre-Test 1 (Units 1 - 6)

(A) Add **a** or **an**.

1 .... egg **2** .... ball **3** .... doll **4** .... umbrella

5 .... nurse **6** .... octopus **7** .... lamb **8** .... elephant

(B) Write the numbers as in the example.

Example: * * *   three

9 * * * * * * * * *   ....   **11** * * * * * * * * *   ....
10 * * * * * * *   ....   **12** * * * * * * * * * * *   ....

(C) Fill in the plural form.

13 one fly — two ....   **14** one witch — two ....

15 one brush — two ....   **16** one man — two ....

17 one tooth — two ....   **18** one mouse — two ....

19 one girl — two ....

20 one ostrich — two ....

D Fill in: he, she, it or they.

21 John .... **23** Sally .... **25** jam ....
22 chairs .... **24** mice .... **26** policeman ....

E Fill in: is or are.

Mark **27)** .... a policeman. He **28)** .... from London. He **29)** ....
twenty-six. Alain **30)** .... a doctor. He **31)** .... from France. Sally and
Julie **32)** .... from England. They **33)** .... students. Hans and Freda
34) .... from Germany. They **35)** .... twenty. They **36)** .... dancers.

F Answer the questions.

37 Is he a pilot?

....

....

38 Is she a singer?

....

....

39 Are they teachers?

....

....

40 Are they pilots?

....

....

Pre-Test 2 (Units 1 - 10)

A Fill in: have, has, is, are or can.

Ann **1)** .... got blonde hair and blue eyes. She **2)** .... thirteen. She **3)** .... a pupil. She **4)** .... dance and sing. Tom and Sally **5)** .... got black hair and green eyes. They **6)** .... twenty-nine. They **7)** .... teachers. They **8)** .... drive a car and play tennis.

B Fill in: he, she, it or they.

9 David ....   11 woman ....   13 Paul and Tom ....
10 books ....   12 sofa ....   14 fireman ....

C Write the plural forms.

15 tooth ....   17 man ....   19 bus ....
16 boy ....   18 cow ....   20 girl ....

D Write the numbers.

21 * * * * * * * * *   ....
22 * *   ....
23 * * * * * * * * * * * *   ....
24 * * * * * * * * * * *   ....

E Write what there is in the living-room.

25 (sofas) ....
....
26 (armchair) ....
....
27 (table) ....
....
28 (pictures) ....
....
29 (woman) ....
....

F **Answer with:** Yes, she has / No, she hasn't **or** Yes, she can / No, she can't.

long hair	can swim
big eyes	can't drive
small nose	
big mouth	

30 Has she got long hair? ....

31 Has she got small eyes? ....

32 Has she got a big nose? ....

33 Has she got a small mouth? ....

34 Can she swim? ....

35 Can she drive? ....

G **Fill in:** this, that, these **or** those.

36 .... is ☞ a watermelon and .... is ☞ an orange.

37 .... are ☞ lemons and .... are ☞ strawberries.

38 .... are ☞ pineapples and .... are ☞ grapes.

39 .... is ☞ an apple and .... is ☞ a melon.

40 .... are ☞ tomatoes and .... are ☞ cherries.

Pre-Test 3 (Units 1 - 14)

A Look at the pictures, then write about picture B.

1   There is a tree.
2   A man is standing under the tree.
3   A child is eating a banana.
4   A woman is making a sandwich.
5   The dog has got a ball in its mouth.

1   ....
2   ....
3   ....
4   ....
5   ....

B Rewrite the text changing the underlined words with *personal pronouns* or *possessive adjectives*.

John is making a sandwich. **6)** John's brother is sitting under a tree. A bird is in the tree. **7)** The bird is singing. John's parents are sitting on the grass. **8)** John's parents are drinking coffee. **9)** John's brother is eating a banana.

....
....
....
....
....

C Fill in: have, has, is, am or can.

Hello! I **10)** .... Clive, the clown. I **11)** .... got a dog, Bonzo. He **12)** .... very clever. He **13)** .... ride a bicycle. He **14)** .... got a hat on his head.

D Fill the blanks with one of the verbs from the box.

open	eat	tidy

15 .... your room!   16 .... the door, please!   17 .... your food!

E Write what there is in the picture.

18 (children) ....

....

19 (birthday cake) ....

....

20 (balloons)..

....

21 (clown) ....

....

F Choose the correct item.

22 Look at those ....!
    A) fly   **B)** flies   **C)** fly's

23 I'm John and this is .... pet dog.
    A) my   **B)** our   **C)** his

24 She .... to the park every day.
    A) is going   **B)** go   **C)** goes

25 This is Bob and Tom and these are
    .... bikes.
    A) my   **B)** their   **C)** our

26 He .... like eggs.
    A) doesn't   **B)** do not   **C)** don't

G **Read the text then answer the questions.**

My name is Sue. I like dancing. I can't speak French. Look! I've got flowers.

27 Is her name Ann?

....

28 Does she like dancing?

....

29 Can she speak French?

....

30 Has she got flowers?

....

H **Fill in with *Present Simple* or *Present Continuous*.**

Ann is a doctor. She **31)** .... **(work)** in a hospital but today she **32)** .... **(stay)** at home. Look! She **33)** .... **(cook)** dinner. Her friends **34)** .... **(visit)** her today. It **35)** .... **(be)** her birthday.

I **Fill in with *Present Simple* or *Present Continuous*.**

Billy: Hello Tom. Where **36)** .... **(you/go)**?

Tom: To school. I usually **37)** .... **(walk)** but today I **38)** .... **(ride)** my new bike. **39)** .... **(you/like)** it? It **40)** .... **(be)** my birthday present.

Billy: Oh! It's a great bike.

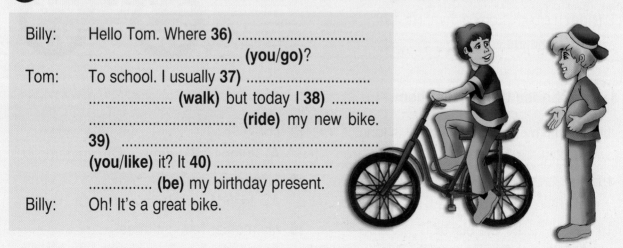

Pre-Test 4 (Units 1 - 17)

A Fill in: on, in, under or behind.

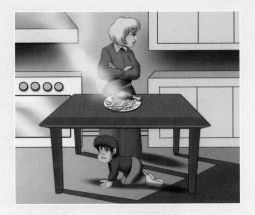

There's a table **1)** .... the kitchen. There is a plate **2)** .... the table. John's mum is **3)** .... the table. She can't find John. He's **4)** .... the table. He doesn't want to eat his chicken.

B Fill in: who or what.

Sam: **5)** ....'s that in your hand, Kitty?
Kitty: It's a photo. Look!
Sam: **6)** ....'s that boy?
Kitty: He's my friend, Nick.
Sam: **7)** ....'s that?
Kitty: It's Nick's bike. I like it very much.
Sam: **8)** ....'s that girl on the bike?
Kitty: That's me.

C Fill in with *Present Simple* or *Present Continuous*.

This **9)** .... **(be)** John Ford. He **10)** .... **(be)** a very rich man. He usually **11)** .... **(drive)** his Rolls Royce but today he **12)** .... **(ride)** his bike. Look at him! He **13)** .... **(eat)** a banana.

D Choose the correct item.

14 This is my cat. .... tail is long.
  A) It   **B)** Its   **C)** Their

15 She .... got a beautiful house.
  A) has   **B)** have   **C)** don't have

16 .... he like biscuits?
  A) Does   **B)** Do   **C)** Don't

17 Look! They .... into the water.
  A) jumps   **B)** jump   **C)** are jumping

18 This is my .... bike.
  A) friends   **B)** friend   **C)** friend's

19 My mother has got three ....
  A) child   **B)** children   **C)** child's

20 .... talk! I'm studying.
   A) Doesn't **B)** Don't **C)** Not

21 "Who .... you?" "I'm John"
   A) are   **B)** is   **C)** am

22 "Can you drive a car?" "No, I ...."
   A) don't **B)** can't **C)** haven't

23 This is .... octopus.
   A) a   **B)** that   **C)** an

E **Fill in with *Present Simple* or *Continuous*.**

Jane: What **24)** .... **(you/do)**?
Paula: I **25)** .... **(tidy)** the living room.
      Simon usually **26)** .... **(clean)** it
      on Tuesdays but today he's ill.
Jane: That's OK. Simon usually **27)** ....
      (cook) today but I **28)** ....
      (cook) for him.

F **Read the text and then write the questions to the short answers.**

Phin is a dolphin. He swims in the pool. He has got two friends. The children love Phin. Phin loves children. He can jump very high.

29 ....? No, he isn't.
30 ....? Yes, he does.
31 ....? No, he hasn't.
32 ....? Yes, they do.
33 ....? Yes, he does.
34 ....? No, he can't.

G **Write what there is in the picture.**

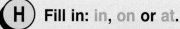

35 ....

36 ....

37 ....

H **Fill in: in, on or at.**

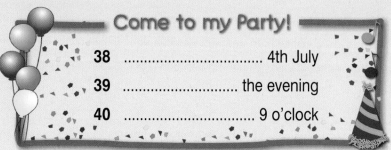

Come to my Party!

38 .... 4th July

39 .... the evening

40 .... 9 o'clock

Progress Tests

Progress Test 1 (Units 1 - 2)

NAME: .... DATE: ....

CLASS: .... MARK: ....

(Time: 30 minutes)

A Write in capital letters.

e.g. apple   *APPLE*

  1 cat   ....
  2 purse   ....

  3 kite   ....
  4 train   ....
  5 umbrella ....

B Correct the words.

e.g. jamb *lamb*

6 mam ....

7 dook ....

8 lish ....

9 nabbit ....

10 besk ....

C Circle the odd letter.

e.g. e e e (a) e e

  11 s s c s s s
  12 d d b d d d

  13 q q q q p q
  14 m m m m n m
  15 g q g g g g

95

D Fill in: a or an.

e.g. *an* elephant

18 .... apple

16 .... dog

19 .... hat

17 .... watch

20 .... ice cream

Progress Test 2 (Units 3 - 4)

NAME: ....   DATE: ....

CLASS: ....   MARK: ....

(Time: 30 minutes)

(A) **Count the stars and write the numbers.**

e.g. *****   *five*

1 ***   ....

2 ******   ....

3 **********   ....

4 ****   ....

5 ************   ....

(B) **Fill in the plural, as in the example.**

e.g. One bus. Two *buses*.

6 One tomato. Two ....

7 One woman. Two ....

8 One bird. Two ....

9 One mouse. Two ....

10 One sheep. Two ....

C **Write the plural form.**

e.g. lion   *lions*

11 child   ....

12 man   ....

13 spy   ....

14 goose   ....

15 fish   ....

D **Write what you can see in the picture.**

e.g. *a/one* house

16 .... birds

17 .... dogs

18 .... cow

19 .... goats

20 .... trees

Progress Test 3 (Units 5 - 6)

NAME: .... DATE: ....

CLASS: .... MARK: ....

(Time: 30 minutes)

A **Fill in:** I, he, she, it, we **or** they.

e.g. *he*

3 ....

1 ....

4 ....

2 ....

5 ....

B **Fill in:** he, she, it, we **or** they.

e.g. dogs *they*

6 John ....

7 Sarah ....

8 Tom and Jane ....

9 cat ....

10 Paul and I ....

C **Answer the questions, as in the example.**

e.g. Are they
policemen?
...No, they aren't.
They are firemen.

11 Is he a teacher?
....
....
....

12 Is she a doctor?
....
....
....

99

13 Are they singers?

....

....

....

14 Are they acrobats?

....

....

....

15 Is he a fireman?

....

....

....

D Write the plural.

e.g. It is a flower.

...*They are flowers*...

16 She is a teacher.

....

....

17 It is a tree.

....

....

18 I am a child.

....

....

19 He is a man.

....

....

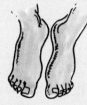

20 It is a foot.

....

....

Progress Test 4 (Units 7 - 8)

NAME: .... DATE: ....

CLASS: .... MARK: ....

(Time: 30 minutes)

A **Fill in:** this, that, these **or** those.

e.g. *This* is ☞ 🍎 an apple and *that* is ☞ 🍊 an orange.

1 .... is ☞ a doll and .... is ☞ a ball.

2 .... are ☞ grapes and .... are ☞ cherries.

3 .... are ☞ books and .... are ☞ pens.

4 .... is ☞ a girl and .... is ☞ a boy.

5 .... are ☞ onions and .... are ☞ carrots.

B **Write sentences using** that **or** those.

e.g. ...*That is a bus.*

6 ....

7 ....

8 ....

9 ....

10 ....

C **Write short answers.**

 jumper ✓

 jeans ✓

 watch ✗

 doll ✗

 bike ✓

 balloon ✗

e.g. Have you got a jumper?
Yes, I have.

11 Have you got jeans?
....

12 Have you got a watch?
....

13 Have you got a doll?
....

14 Have you got a bike?
....

15 Have you got a balloon?
....

D **Write what Ann has got.**

curly blonde hair	small nose
big blue eyes	beautiful face
big mouth	green T-shirt

e.g. ...*Ann has got curly blonde hair....*

16 ....

17 ....

18 ....

19 ....

20 ....

Progress Test 5 (Units 9 - 10)

NAME: .... DATE: ....

CLASS: .... MARK: ....

(Time: 30 minutes)

A **Write what there is in the picture.**

e.g. (bird) ...*There are two birds*....

1 (woman) ....
2 (boy) ....
3 (dog) ....
4 (tree) ....
5 (banana) ....

B **Look at the picture and answer the questions.**

e.g. Is there a wolf in the picture?   ...*Yes, there is*....

6 Is there a dog in the picture?   ....
7 Are there birds in the picture?   ....
8 Is there a rabbit in the picture?   ....
9 Are there houses in the picture?   ....
10 Are there trees in the picture?   ....

C **Answer the questions, as in the example.**

e.g. Can you see a dog?   ...*Yes, I can*....

11 Can you see a postman? ....
12 Can you see a car?   ....
13 Can you see a bag?   ....
14 Can you see a ball?   ....
15 Can you see letters?   ....

103

D True or False?

e.g. Fish can read. ...*False. Fish can't read*....

16 Birds can drive. ....

17 Dogs can run. ....

18 Elephants can cook. ....

19 Rabbits can jump. ....

20 Monkeys can climb. ....

Progress Test 6 (Units 11 - 12)

NAME: .... DATE: ....

CLASS: .... MARK: ....

(Time: 30 minutes)

 A **Fill in:** my, your, his, her, its, our **or** their.

e.g. He's got a book.
It's ...*his*... book.

1 You've got a car.
It's .... car.

2 They've got a cat.
It's .... cat.

3 He's got a computer.
It's .... computer.

4 She's got a bag.
It's .... bag.

5 I've got a bike.
It's .... bike.

B **Rewrite the sentences changing the underlined words.**

This is <u>David's</u> bedroom. This is <u>David's</u> mother. <u>His mother's</u> name is Sandra. <u>Sandra's</u> hair is blonde. <u>David's</u> pyjamas are red. Sandra wants David to get up because <u>Sandra and David's</u> breakfast is ready.

e.g. ...*This is his bedroom*....

6 ....

7 ....

8 ....

9 ....

10 ....

Match the sentences with the pictures.

Tidy your room.	Wake up.	Go to bed.
Drink your milk!	Do your homework.	Brush your teeth!

e.g. ...*Wake up*...

11 ....
....

12 ....
....

13 ....
....

14 ....
....

15 ....
....

D **Write the negative form.**

e.g. Run!   *Don't run!*

16 Sit down! ....

17 Do your homework! ....

18 Open the door! ....

19 Eat your dinner! ....

20 Go to bed! ....

Progress Test 7 (Units 13 - 14)

NAME: .... DATE: ....

CLASS: .... MARK: ....

(Time: 30 minutes)

A Fill in: am, is or are.

e.g. She ...is... doing her homework.

1 They .... walking.
2 I .... drinking milk.

3 You .... watching TV.
4 He .... cooking the dinner.
5 It .... sleeping.

B Look at the picture and answer yes or no.

e.g. Is Sally sitting on the floor? ...Yes, she is.

6 Is Dad reading a book? ....
7 Is Mum cooking the dinner? ....
8 Is Sally watching TV? ....
9 Are Ann and Nick doing their homework? ....
10 Is Dad sleeping? ....

C Write the 3rd person singular.

e.g. I walk - he ...walks...

11 I have - he ....
12 I do - she ....

13 I study - he ....
14 I play - she ....
15 I wash - he ....

D **Put the verbs in the correct tense.**

e.g. a) I usually ...*wear*... **(wear)** old clothes.

　　 b) Today, I ...*am wearing*... **(wear)** a beautiful dress.

16 a) She usually .... **(go)** to work by bus.
　　 b) Today, she .... **(go)** to work by car.

17 a) We usually .... **(eat)** dinner at seven o'clock.
　　 b) Today, we .... **(eat)** dinner at eight o'clock.

18 a) He .... **(do)** his homework now.
　　 b) He .... **(do)** his homework every day.

19 a) I .... **(drink)** coffee now.
　　 b) I .... **(drink)** tea every morning.

20 a) They usually .... **(play)** football.
　　 b) Today, they .... **(play)** tennis.

Progress Test 8 (Units 15 - 17)

NAME: ....   DATE: ....

CLASS: ....   MARK: ....

(Time: 30 minutes)

A **Fill in:** in, on, behind **or** under.

Dad is asleep ...*under*... a tree. There are two birds **1)** .... the tree. Rover, our dog, is asleep **2)** .... the grass. Sam is standing **3)** .... the birds. There are some peaches and bananas **4)** .... the blanket. There is a goose **5)** .... a tree.

B **Fill in:** in, on **or** at.

e.g. ...*in*... November

6 .... 10 o'clock

7 .... Monday

8 .... the afternoon

9 .... Easter

10 .... summer

Match up the sentences.

e.g. What is that?   *It's a rabbit.*

11 Who are they?   **a** They're strawberries.
12 What are you doing?   **b** It's a book.
13 What are these?   **c** He's Ben.
14 Who is he?   **d** They're my friends.
15 What is this?   **e** I'm watching TV.

 Fill in: in, on or at.

This is Sue. She lives ...*in*... a big house. She gets up **16)** .... seven o'clock **17)** ....
the morning and swims **18)** .... the pool. Then she goes to work. She comes home
19) .... five o'clock. **20)** .... Saturdays and Sundays she visits her friends.